Living in Alaska

Lisa Shulman

A Harcourt Achieve Imprint

www.Rigby.com
1-800-531-5015

This is Alaska.

Alaska is a state.

It is summer
in Alaska.
It is time to go
to sleep.
The sun is in the sky.

It is winter in Alaska.
It is time to go
to school.
The moon is
in the sky.

It is summer
in Alaska.
It is time to play
in the sun.

It is winter in Alaska.
It is time to play
in the snow.

It is summer
in Alaska.
It is fun
to pick berries.

It is winter in Alaska.
It is fun to look up
at the sky.

It is fun to live
in Alaska!